PEOPLE YOU
SHOULD KNOW

DOLORES HUERTA

Get to Know the Voice of Migrant Workers

by Robert Liu-Trujillo

Consultant: Fred Glass
Author, *From Mission to Microchip: A History of the California Labor Movement*
Berkeley, California

CAPSTONE PRESS
a capstone imprint

Fact Finders Books are published by Capstone Press
1710 Roe Crest Drive, North Mankato, Minnesota 56003
www.capstonepub.com

**Library of Congress Cataloging-in-Publication data is available
on the Library of Congress website.**

ISBN 978-1-5435-7181-3 (hardcover)
ISBN 978-1-5435-7463-0 (paperback)
ISBN 978-1-5435-7188-2 (eBook PDF)

Editorial Credits
Mari Bolte, editor; Kayla Rossow, designer; Tracy Cummins, media researcher;
Tori Abraham, production specialist

Photo Credits
Alamy: Pictures Now, 12; AP Photo: 15, 25; Getty Images: Arthur Schatz/The LIFE Picture Collection, 5, Bettmann, 17, Cathy Murphy, 6, 21, 26, Denver Post, 9; Newscom: Adrian Mendoza 040182008/ Modesto Bee/ZUMAPRESS.com, 11, Johns PKI/Splash News, 29; The Image Works: © 1976 George Ballis/Take Stock, Cover, 23; Walter P. Reuther Library/Archives of Labor and Urban Affairs, Wayne State University, 18

Source Notes
p. 6, line 2: United Farm Workers. "The History of Si Se Puede." https://ufw.org/research/history/history-si-se-puede. Accessed February 1, 2019.

p. 7, fact box: Maria Godoy. "Dolores Huerta: The Civil Rights Icon Who Showed Farmworkers 'Si Se Puede.'" https://www.wgbh.org/news/2017/09/17/dolores-huerta-civil-rights-icon-who-showed-farmworkers-si-se-puede. Accessed November 5, 2018.

p. 10, line 10: *A Dolores Huerta Reader.* ed. Mario T. Garcia. Albuquerque: University of New Mexico Press, 2008, page 9.

p. 16, line 7: Maria Godoy.

p. 19, sidebar: Hillary Haenes. "My Inspiration: Dolores Huerta and Her Daughters." https://www.bakersfield.com/news/health/my-inspiration-dolores-huerta-her-daughters/article_68193ca0-8b07-5b03-95fa-b4070bdf3bea.html. Accessed December 13, 2018.

p. 21, fact box: Julia Bencomo Lobaco. "Dolores Huerta: The Vision and Voice of Her Life's Work." https://www.aarp.org/politics-society/history/info-2004/interview_dolores_hurerta.html. Accessed December 11, 2018.

p. 22, line 12: "Coachella Valley: Filipino's 1965 Strike Set Stage for Farm Labor Cause." https://www.pe.com/2005/09/03/coachella-valley-filipinos-1965-strike-set-stage-for-farm-labor-cause/. Accessed December 13, 2018.

p. 27, line 9: Molly Boyle. "The Power Is in Your Body: The Activism of Dolores Huerta." http://www.santafenewmexican.com/pasatiempo/the-power-is-in-your-body-the-activism-of-dolores/article_4a3dab3e-72f0-5d39-9248-edd56a196c9c.html. Accessed December 13, 2018.

All internet sites appearing in back matter were available and accurate when this book was sent to press.

Printed in the United States of America.
PA70

TABLE OF CONTENTS

1

¡SÍ, SE PUEDE!

Dolores Huerta had long been a voice for farm workers. She wanted them to work together and form a **union**. She wanted their voices to be heard.

Large farms in central California relied on thousands of farm workers to grow and harvest their crops. The food they grew was sold around the country. But the workers were treated poorly. They worked from sunup to sundown without shade, cold drinking water, or rest breaks. There were no bathrooms nearby. And despite working so hard, workers in the southwest United States only earned between 70 cents and $1.65 an hour.

Dolores and Cesar would work together for more than 30 years.

It was May 1972. Dolores and her colleague Cesar Chavez had traveled to Arizona to speak with politicians about a recent bill that had just been passed. In it, farm workers would no longer have the right to **strike** and **boycott**. Their voices would be crushed.

boycott—to refuse to take part in something as a way of making a protest

strike—to refuse to work because of a disagreement with the employer over wages or working conditions

union—an organized group of workers that tries to gain better pay and working conditions for workers

Dolores stands in front of the flag representing the United Farm Workers union. Dolores and Cesar co-founded the group. The motto, *Viva la Causa*, means "long live the cause."

Governor Jack Williams refused to see them. "As far as I'm concerned, those people don't exist," he said. But local union leaders did meet with Dolores and Cesar.

The union leaders explained that the companies that owned the farms were very powerful. They had connections with politicians, police officers, and judges who would quickly side with them. Fighting them would never work. "No, no, *se puede*," they said. "No, no, it can't be done."

Dolores stood. "No," she said. "In Arizona *sí, se puede!*" Yes, we can! *Sí, se puede* became the rallying cry of the farm worker's movement in Arizona. Since that day, activists around the country have answered that call.

DID YOU KNOW?

"That became the slogan of our campaign in Arizona and now is the slogan for the immigrant rights movement . . . We can do it. I can do it. Sí se puede."
—Dolores Huerta

2

EARLY LIFE

Dolores Clara Fernandez was born on April 10, 1930, in Dawson, New Mexico. Her parents, Juan Fernandez and Alicia Chavez, divorced when she was young. Alicia, Dolores, and Dolores's brothers moved to Stockton, California.

Dolores was always talkative and persuasive. Her grandfather, who helped raise Dolores, called her "*Siete Lenguas*," or Seven Tongues, because she talked so much.

Although she didn't see her father often, his actions influenced her early on. He was a farm worker and miner. He was also an **activist**. He was a member of the miner's union in New Mexico. The mine owners **blacklisted** him because of his active participation in the union. In 1938 he was elected to the New Mexico State **Legislature**. He used his position to fight for workers' rights.

Enemies in High Places

Juan was a well-respected member of the New Mexico Legislature. He was expelled before his term was up because he had an argument with a prominent New Mexico farm owner. The owner employed a lot of farm workers and had a lot of influence. He would later become a congressman.

The mining community of Dawson, New Mexico, in the 1950s. The mine was closed shortly after, and the town was abandoned.

DID YOU KNOW?

Dolores is a fifth-generation American. Her great-grandfather fought in the Civil War (1861–1865).

activist—person who works for social or political change

blacklisted—to be barred from employment for holding undesired opinions

legislature—a group of people in the federal or state government that has the power to make or pass laws

Alicia ran a restaurant during the day and worked in a cannery at night. She later bought and ran a hotel. Dolores and her siblings helped their mother by cleaning and doing the laundry. Many of the hotel patrons were low-wage workers. Alicia would often let them stay for free because she knew they were struggling to get by.

Alicia encouraged Dolores to try new things. "My mother was always pushing me to get involved in all these youth activities," Dolores said. Dolores took piano and violin lessons. She studied ballet, tap, and *folklorico*, traditional Mexican dances. She joined her church's youth group and choir, and she was an active Girl Scout.

Dolores's community was made up of diverse groups of people, including Chinese, Filipino, African American, and Hispanic people. Her troop represented that. Dolores was a Girl Scout from age 8 to age 18.

Today the Girl Scouts of America offers the Dolores Huerta Girl Scout Patch. Scouts must learn about Dolores and give a presentation about her life and her work.

Dolores graduated from Stockton High School in 1947.

Dolores stayed active, joining many school clubs at Stockton High School. During this time, she began to notice that nonwhite people were treated badly. Sometimes her friends would be bothered, especially when they gathered in mixed groups. Dolores created a safe space for those friends to meet at a family friend's store. She wanted them to be able to get together without being harassed.

Dolores also became aware of how little support Hispanic and African American students received. Many became frustrated and dropped out of school. The ones who stayed were discouraged from taking classes that would prepare them for college. She experienced that frustration herself when one of her teachers accused her of cheating on a test. He refused to believe she could write well.

3

WORK BEFORE SCHOOL

After high school, Dolores attended college in Stockton. She wanted to be a teacher. She also married Ralph Head and had two daughters. The marriage did not last long.

Dolores began teaching elementary school in California in the early 1950s. Many of her students were the children of farm workers. They came to school hungry, dirty, and in worn-out clothes. Sometimes they didn't stay for the whole year. Their parents had to move to find work in other cities or states. Having such a **disruptive** home life made learning very difficult.

disruptive—causing difficulties that interrupt or prevent something

Between 1942 and 1964, more than 4.6 million individual Bracero contracts were signed.

The Bracero Program

During World War II (1939–1945) Mexico and the United States started the Bracero Program. Mexican men were invited to sign short-term contracts to work in the United States, mostly for agricultural jobs. The program was meant to be temporary, to fill labor shortages caused by American men going off to war. But it lasted much longer than that.

Employers were supposed to pay fair wages and provide good housing and food, insurance, and transportation back to Mexico. They were also not supposed to be able to work as strikebreakers. But often these rules were ignored. The growers increased their profits while ignoring strikers and keeping their labor costs as low as possible.

Dolores tried to get food **vouchers** for her students so they could eat. She tried to get clothing vouchers so they could have decent shoes. But the principal didn't believe the students deserved help.

Dolores knew that wasn't true. She had been around farm workers all her life. "When I saw people in their homes—they had dirt floors. And the furniture was orange crates and cardboard boxes. People were so incredibly poor and they were working so hard . . . you saw how hard they were working, and yet they were not getting paid anything." She decided she needed to help the parents to help the children.

Farm labor laws do not always protect agricultural workers. For example, overtime pay, minimum wage, and health and disability insurance are not always guaranteed. Workers also may face consequences for joining a union.

Working the Fields

Migrant workers still must follow the crops to find work. One week they might pick cotton in Texas. The next, they could travel to Indiana to harvest tomatoes. Another week might find them in California picking grapes. The work is backbreaking, often done in the hot sun with no shade. They work 10 hours a day, seven days a week. Children work in the fields too. Some are as young as seven. In 2017 experts estimated that about 500,000 farm workers were under 18 years old.

migrant worker—a person who travels from place to place in search of work

voucher—a coupon that entitles the holder to discounted or free goods or services

4

THE REAL WORK BEGINS

In 1955 25-year-old Dolores joined the Community Service Organization (CSO). CSO was a **civil rights** organization dedicated to fighting **discrimination** and police abuse. It also encouraged people to vote. Dolores ran CSO's **civic** and educational programs. During this time she learned valuable lessons about community organizing.

Founding members of the CSO in the 1950s. Cesar Chavez is second from the right.

Organizing farm workers was not one of the group's main goals. But Dolores soon met national staff director Cesar Chavez. The son of migrant workers, Cesar had been a community organizer with the group for years. His job had led him to speak to Latin Americans, including farm workers, around California. He knew the troubles they faced in the fields. In 1962 Cesar had asked group leaders to let him organize a labor union. They turned him down.

Work First

Dolores married fellow activist Ventura Huerta in the early 1950s. They had five children together. Some believe they divorced because Ventura thought Dolores spent too much time with CSO and not enough time at home.

"We witnessed all the adversity, challenges, and just plain 'hate' our mother faced, and I would think, when will she give it up and say, 'Enough!' Well, she has never given up and she continues to be strong for all people," her daughter Angela has said.

civic—relating to citizenship

civil rights—the rights that all people have to freedom and equal treatment under the law

discrimination—the practice of treating a person or group of people differently and unfairly when compared with another group

Cesar and Dolores left CSO and co-founded the National Farm Workers Association (NFWA) in 1962.

Dolores spent her time **lobbying** in Sacramento. She wanted to change laws to protect farm workers. One law, Aid for Dependent Families, made disability insurance for farm workers possible. She also helped get the **minimum wage** for field workers raised to $1.60 an hour.

While Dolores worked behind the scenes, Cesar became the face of the organization. He traveled around California speaking to farm workers about how joining together in a union would help everyone. He made everyone feel that they were important and that their thoughts and opinions mattered. By 1970 the union had 50,000 members.

lobby—to try to persuade government officials to act or vote in a certain way
minimum wage—the lowest amount a company can legally pay a worker

Dolores had to fight against sexism too. During union meetings, she would mark every time someone made a sexist comment. At the end of the meeting, she would announce how many had been made.

DID YOU KNOW?

Cesar and Dolores didn't always see eye to eye. But they respected each other, even when they disagreed. "I told him, 'I feel so bad when I fight with you.' He said, 'Don't ever stop. Don't ever stop fighting with me. You're the one that really helps me think.'"

On September 8, 1965, members of the Agricultural Workers Organizing Committee (AWOC) went on strike. Several thousand workers across at least 20 different grape farms walked off the job. Made up of Filipino American, Mexican, and black workers, and led by Larry Itliong, they were fighting for better pay.

Cesar and Dolores had been planning a strike too, but had wanted to wait until their organization was larger. Still, they knew joining Larry would help both groups. "They set the stage for everything," Cesar's son Paul said later. "Nobody showed the kind of conviction these men did."

DID YOU KNOW?

The NFWA and AWOC merged in 1966 to become the United Farm Workers Organizing Committee (UFWOC). In 1970 the name was changed to the United Farm Workers of America.

Dolores (far right) and Cesar at a strike meeting in 1966. By the end of the summer, workers from more than 30 farms had joined them.

On September 16 NFWA voted to join the strike. Dolores organized 5,000 workers to participate. Other workers and volunteers picketed. The strike lasted for years. When the union signed a contract with grape growers in 1970, Dolores was the main force behind negotiations. Union members finally had better pay, job benefits, and worker protections.

In 1973 Dolores's rallying cry of "¡Sí, Se Puede!" led to another boycott. By this time, the three-year contracts UFW signed in 1970 had expired. Growers used this time to sign "sweetheart" deals with another union. These deals often favored the growers and gave the workers little in return. Dolores's group was not a part of this union, but the deals were signed as if they were.

Unionized grape and lettuce workers held strikes across California. Thousands of nonviolent strikers were attacked or arrested. Two were killed. Cesar was arrested. But Dolores and her supporters spread the word. By 1975 17 million Americans were boycotting non-union grapes, lettuce, and Gallo brand wine, which was made in California.

The Agricultural Labor Relations Act was passed that year. It gave farm workers in California the right to assemble, organize, and negotiate union contracts with their employers.

Dolores continued her work for human rights. In 1988 she attended a peaceful protest in San Francisco. The 1,000 protesters objected to vice president George H.W. Bush's opposition to the boycott. Dolores was handing out leaflets on UFW's grape boycott.

A policeman swung his baton at Dolores. The 5-foot-tall 58-year-old grandmother was rushed to the hospital. She had several broken ribs and a ruptured spleen, which had to be removed.

Dolores was arrested more than 20 times in her life.

Dolores has said that she wasn't meant to be a housewife—she was meant to be an activist. She began a relationship with Cesar's brother Richard in the late 1960s or early 1970s. It lasted more than 40 years. Together they had four children.

Dolores and three of her seven daughters in the mid–1970s.

Sometimes she was called out for being more of an activist than a mother. She attended rallies and protests while pregnant. She changed diapers and nursed babies between meetings.

Her children have said that when they were young they did not always know why she put her work first. But as adults, they understand. "We soon realized that my mother didn't really belong to us," her son Emilio said.

Dangerous Fields

Dolores always felt that human rights were a family matter. After all, families spent hours together working in the fields. When they protested, they protested together. The **pesticides** used by the growers affected families too. Exposure to the chemicals in pesticides can cause nausea, breathing problems, and other long-term illnesses such as lung cancer. They can also cause birth defects. The danger was everyone's.

pesticide—poisonous chemicals used to kill insects, rodents, and fungi that can damage plants

Cesar died in 1993. Instead of taking over the union, Dolores, in her early 60s at that time, decided to step down. She spent time with her family. She also continued her humanitarian work, traveling the country with a group called the Feminist Majority's Feminization of Power. The group's goal is to work toward women's equality, both on the street and in politics. Dolores worked to get more Latinas elected into office.

Dolores won the Puffin/Nation Prize for Creative Citizenship in 2002. She used the $100,000 award money to found the Dolores Huerta Foundation. The foundation works to engage and develop natural leaders, teaching them how to speak up through community organizing, leadership, and civic engagement. The foundation is located in Bakersfield, California, where Dolores grew up.

President Barack Obama awarded Dolores the Presidential Medal of Freedom in 2012. This is the highest award a civilian can be given. Obama had used Dolores's slogan for his presidential campaign: Yes, We Can!

In 2017 a documentary titled *Dolores* was released. Its intent was to give Dolores equal credit with Cesar Chavez for the formation and growth of the UFW.

Dolores, at 88 years old, spent 2018 knocking on doors and registering voters. That year's Congress had 42 Latino members—a record number. ¡Sí, Se Puede!

GLOSSARY

activist (AK-tuh-vist)—a person who works for social or political change

blacklisted (BLAK-lisst-ed)—to be barred from employment for holding undesired opinions

boycott (BOY-kot)—to refuse to take part in something as a way of making a protest

civic (SIV-ik)—relating to citizenship

civil rights (SI-vil RYTS)—the rights that all people have to freedom and equal treatment under the law

discrimination (dis-kri-muh-NAY-shuhn)—the practice of treating a person or group of people differently and unfairly when compared with another group

disruptive (dis-RUP-tihv)—causing difficulties that interrupt or prevent something

legislature (LEJ-is-lay-chur)—a group of people in the federal or state government that has the power to make or pass laws

lobby (LOB-ee)—to try to persuade government officials to act or vote in a certain way

migrant worker (MYE-gruhnt WURK-uhr)—person who travels from place to place in search of work

minimum wage (MIN-uh-muhm WAJE)—the lowest amount a company can legally pay a worker

pesticide (PESS-duh-syde)—poisonous chemicals used to kill insects, rodents, and fungi that can damage plants

sexism (SEKS-iz-uhm)—discrimination based on whether a person is male or female

strike (STRIKE)—to refuse to work because of a disagreement with the employer over wages or working conditions

union (YOON-yuhn)—an organized group of workers that tries to gain better pay and working conditions for workers

voucher (VOW-chur)—a coupon that entitles the holder to discounted or free goods or services

READ MORE

Barghoorn, Linda. *Dolores Huerta: Advocate for Women and Workers*. New York: Crabtree Publishing Company, 2017.

Langston-George, Rebecca. *Cesar Chavez: Get to Know the Leader Who Won Rights for Workers*. Mankato, MN: Capstone Press, 2019.

Yasuda, Anita. *Children Working the Fields*. Lake Elmo, MN: Focus Readers, 2019.

INTERNET SITES

Dolores Huerta Foundation
http://doloreshuerta.org/dolores-huerta/

National Women's History Museum: Dolores Huerta
https://www.womenshistory.org/education-resources/biographies/dolores-huerta

United Farm Workers
https://ufw.org/

CRITICAL THINKING QUESTIONS

1. Choose one event in Dolores's early life. How did that event shape her actions as an adult?

2. Dolores wanted to help the children at her school. Are there ways you can help the people in your community? Name at least three ways in which you might help.

3. Dolores and Cesar led strikes, protests, pickets, marches, fasts, and voter registration events. Research one kind of event. Name another time that kind of event has had an effect on history.

INDEX